The White House

by Lisa M. Herrington

Content Consultant

Nanci R. Vargus, Ed.D.
Professor Emeritus, University of Indianapolis

Reading Consultant

Jeanne Clidas, Ph.D.
Reading Specialist

Children's Press®
An Imprint of Scholastic Inc.
New York Toronto London Auckland Sydney
Mexico City New Delhi Hong Kong
Danbury, Connecticut

Library of Congress Cataloging-in-Publication Data
Herrington, Lisa M.
The White House/by Lisa M. Herrington.
    pages cm. — (Rookie read-about American symbols)
Includes bibliographical references and index.
ISBN 978-0-531-21567-8 (library binding: alk. paper) — ISBN 978-0-531-21840-2 (pbk.: alk. paper)
    1. White House (Washington, D.C.)—Juvenile literature. 2. Washington (D.C.)—Buildings, structures, etc.—Juvenile literature. I. Title.

F204.W5H46 2014
975.3—dc23   2014014960

Produced by Spooky Cheetah Press
Design by Keith Plechaty

Printed in China 62

SCHOLASTIC, CHILDREN'S PRESS, ROOKIE READ-ABOUT®, and associated logos are trademarks and/or registered trademarks of Scholastic Inc.

1 2 3 4 5 6 7 8 9 10 R 24 23 22 21 20 19 18 17 16 15

Photographs © 2015: Alamy Images/ZUMA Press: 24; AP Images: 20 (Alex Brandon), 12, 28 right (North Wind Picture Archives), 31 bottom; Corbis Images: 15 (Bettmann), 16 (Pete Souza/White House/CNP); Getty Images: 27 (Mark Wilson), 23, 31 center top (Sharon Farmer/AFP); Media Bakery/John Parrot: 28 left; Reuters/Larry Downing: 19; Shutterstock, Inc./Vacclav: 3 bottom, 29 right, 31 center bottom; The Granger Collection: 8 inset, 29 left, 31 top; The Image Works/Mary Evans: 8 background; Thinkstock: 3 top right (franciscodiazpagador), cover (Gerd Kortemeyer), 4 (igor vorobyov), 3 top left (jim pruitt); White House Historical Association (127): 11.

Illustration p.30 by Jeffrey Chandler/Art Gecko Studios!
Map p.7 by XNR Productions, Inc.

Table of Contents

The President's Home

What is the most famous home in the United States? It is the White House. The president lives and works in the White House. The president's family lives there, too.

The White House is located at 1600 Pennsylvania Avenue.

The White House is surrounded by 18 acres (7 hectares) of land. That is bigger than 13 football fields.

The White House is a famous **symbol**. When people see it, they think of the United States and the president. The White House is in Washington, D.C. That is the country's capital.

FUN FACT!

More than 570 buckets of paint are needed to cover the outside of the White House.

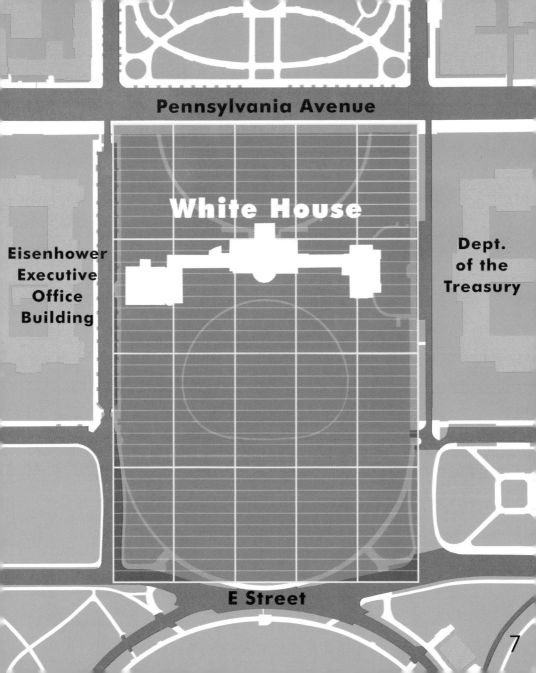

Pennsylvania Avenue

White House

Eisenhower
Executive
Office
Building

Dept.
of the
Treasury

E Street

7

James Hoban

Hoban's sketch for the White House

White House History

George Washington, our first president, chose the spot for the White House. **Architect** James Hoban won a contest to build it.

In 1792, work started on the White House. It took eight years to complete the outside. The walls were made from stone.

John Adams was the second U.S. president. In 1800, he became the first president to live in the White House. At the time, it was called the President's House. The inside had not been finished yet. It was completed in 1809.

FUN FACT!

George Washington is the only president who didn't live in the White House.

In 1814, the United States was at war with Great Britain. British soldiers set fire to the White House. After the fire, only the outside walls remained. By 1817, the White House was rebuilt.

FUN FACT!

First Lady Dolley Madison saved a famous painting of George Washington from the fire. It hangs in the White House today.

Over the years, the White House grew. Porches and two **wings** were added. They are called the West Wing and East Wing. As the years passed, the White House needed repairs. The entire inside was taken out and built again!

FUN FACT!

In 1901, President Theodore Roosevelt gave the White House its name.

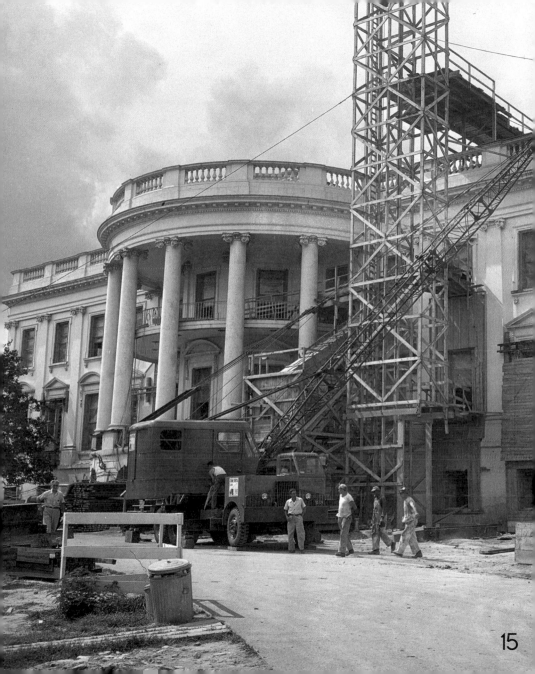

Special Rooms

Today, the White House is huge. It has 132 rooms on six floors. There is a swimming pool, bowling alley, and movie theater.

The President and Mrs. Obama watch the Super Bowl in 3-D in the White House theater.

Some White House rooms are named after colors. The Blue Room has a blue rug, furniture, and curtains. The president meets with guests and world leaders there. There is also a Red Room and a Green Room.

FUN FACT!

The official White House Christmas tree is decorated in the Blue Room.

The East Room is the largest room in the White House. Dances, concerts, and parties take place in the East Room. President Gerald Ford's daughter even had her prom there!

FUN FACT!

Many pets have lived in the White House over the years. They have included dogs, cats, ponies, and even an alligator!

The **Oval Office** is where the president works. The president signs laws and makes speeches there. The Oval Office is also where the president has important meetings. The beautiful Rose Garden is located outside the Oval Office.

The Oval Office is located in the West Wing.

President Bill Clinton

START

The People's House

Many special events are held at the White House. In spring, kids roll Easter eggs on the White House's South Lawn. Kids have also planted vegetables at the White House. And the flower gardens are sometimes open for public tours.

The president may live in the White House, but it is also known as "the People's House."

Each year, the White House welcomes hundreds of thousands of visitors. They can tour certain rooms, see famous paintings, and share in the White House's rich history.

FUN FACT!

The White House is the only home of a country's leader that is regularly open to the public.

Students on a field trip
meet First Lady Laura Bush.

1800
John Adams is the first president to live in the White House.

1814
British soldiers set fire to the White House. Only the outside walls remain.

1792
Workers start to build the White House.

1809
The inside is completed.

1817
The White House is rebuilt.

1901
President Theodore Roosevelt gives the White House its name.

1952
The repairs are done.

Today
The original walls of the White House still stand.

1902
The East Wing and West Wing are added and later made bigger.

1948
The inside of the White House is torn apart.

29

The White House

There are 147 windows and 412 doors in the White House.

The **Blue Room**

The **Lincoln Bedroom** was once President Lincoln's office.

The **East Room** is the largest room in the White House.

The **State Dining Room** can seat 140 people.

Guests meet in the **Diplomatic Room** before big events.

There are more than 2,700 books in the White House **Library**.

Glossary

architect (AR-ki-tekt): person who designs buildings

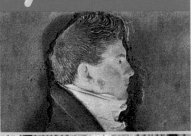

Oval Office (OH-vuhl OF-iss): room in the White House where the president works

symbol (SIM-buhl): object or design that stands for something else

wings (wings): parts of a building that have been added on

Index

Facts for Now

Visit this Scholastic Web site for more information on the White House:
www.factsfornow.scholastic.com
Enter the keywords **White House**

About the Author

Lisa M. Herrington writes books and articles for kids. She lives in Trumbull, Connecticut, with her husband, Ryan, and daughter, Caroline. She has visited the White House twice.